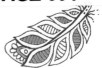
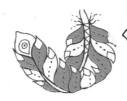

THE
MINDFULNESS
COMPANION

A CREATIVE GUIDE TO BRING CALM TO YOUR DAY

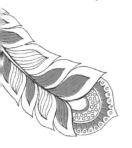
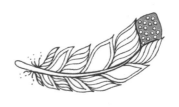
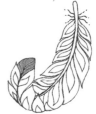

DR. SARAH JANE ARNOLD

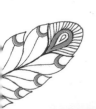

LARK
New York

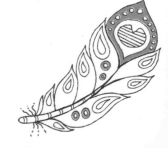

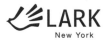

New York

An Imprint of Sterling Publishing
1166 Avenue of the Americas
New York, NY 10036

First published in the United Kingdom in 2016 by Michael O'Mara Books Ltd., as
The Mindfulness Companion: A Creative Journal to Bring Calm to Your Day

ISBN 978-1-4547-1021-9

Distributed in Canada by Sterling Publishing
c/o Canadian Manda Group, 664 Annette Street
Toronto, Ontario, Canada M6S 2C8

For information about custom editions, special sales, and premium
and corporate purchases, please contact Sterling Special Sales at
800-805-5489 or specialsales@sterlingpublishing.com.

Manufactured in China

2 4 6 8 10 9 7 5 3 1

www.sterlingpublishing.com
www.larkcrafts.com

Cover and interior illustrations by Angelea Van Dam
Cover design by Ana Bjezancevic
Designed and typeset by Claire Cater

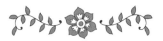

Introducing Mindfulness

Modern life can be busy and demanding. To cope, we plan, strive, work towards our goals, attend to multiple things at once, and go on autopilot to conserve our mental energy and attend to our priorities. This "doing mode" is helpful and positive for us in many respects. It can enable us to progress and achieve the things that we want to do. It is a source of self-esteem. However, *doing* is also associated with the desire for change, dissatisfaction with how things are now, pressure and expectations, the unconscious mind, and learned behaviors. We can be unhelpfully influenced by negative thoughts and challenging feelings when our minds are on autopilot. We may feel drained and incomplete, and forget to appreciate all that we are and all that we have *right now*. Mindfulness offers an accessible way of managing these issues, so that you can achieve a more healthy balance between "doing" and "being" in life.

Mindfulness draws on ancient concepts from Buddhist teachings that are associated with well-being. Simply put, mindfulness means deliberately paying full attention to the present moment, with an attitude of acceptance, kindness, compassion, openness, and curiosity. It is about being in the now, rather than doing for the future. The practice of mindfulness offers you an alternative way of relating to your external

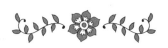

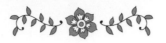

world (your relationships and environment) and your internal experiences (your thoughts, feelings, and bodily sensations) without unhelpful judgements or knee-jerk reactions that can cause distress.

Why Do It?

Western science and psychology have adopted mindfulness because research has found strong evidence that it significantly enhances well-being. For example, mindfulness-based psychological therapy has been found to successfully relieve anxiety disorders, depression, and stress. There is evidence, too, suggesting that mindfulness can be helpful for some people with physical health concerns, such as chronic pain.

It is understood that mindfulness is beneficial for several reasons:

1. Mindfulness encourages you to accept and tolerate challenging emotions, and teaches you not to react in unhelpful ways. A great deal of psychological distress is associated with people trying to suppress or avoid their emotions.
2. Mindfulness supports you to change unhelpful, automatic

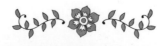

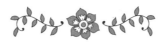

patterns of thinking and responding. When you practice mindful living in the present, your mind dwells less in the past (an aspect of depression) and it gets less caught up in concerns about the future (a feature of anxiety). You learn to view your thoughts as *just thoughts* (that may or may not be true), which you observe from a distance as they enter, stay, and leave your mind. You can then choose if, how, and when you want to respond to them with a more balanced and self-aware mindset.

3. Mindfulness encourages you to be more kind and compassionate to yourself and others. A significant proportion of emotional pain is associated with self-critical thoughts, unhelpful expectations and difficult relationship dynamics.

4. Mindfulness can help you to feel more relaxed and at peace, and accepting of who you are—just as you are. It can promote a sense of appreciation for life and remind you of its wondrous qualities.

It is important to note that you are not aiming for these outcomes while practicing mindfulness; mindfulness is not about striving or wishing that things were different from how they are. However, a positive consequence of practicing mindfulness is that people often find that their well-being increases.

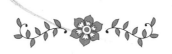

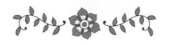

How Do You Do It?

Mindfulness involves learning how to pay attention to your immediate experience of the present moment, just as it is, right now. In order to do this, you can focus on the experience of yourself breathing, your body and bodily sensations, your thoughts, and/or your emotions. You can also focus your attention on your external world, such as what you can see, hear, touch, taste, and smell, moment by moment. Mindfulness is a process of observing, noticing, allowing, and becoming aware of these things, without judging, evaluating, or trying to change your experiences. Mindfulness is also a way of being. When you are being mindful, you take a stance of openness, curiosity, non-judgement, and non-reactivity, and you accept your experiences—just as they are. You may notice that your mind tells you that you do not like some of your experiences, but when practicing mindfulness you accept them, nonetheless, as part of your reality in that moment. When you are being mindful, you also take a stance of self-compassion, and of compassion and loving-kindness towards others. When you feel compassion in this way, you are wishing that you and others are free from suffering. When you feel loving-kindness, you are wishing that you and others are safe, well, and happy, and you extend this love and kindness to all living beings.

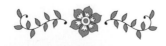

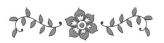

You can practice mindfulness formally and/or informally. Formal mindfulness meditation is when you intentionally take time out from your day, find a quiet space, and then practice mindfulness for a certain amount of time. You typically sit in a comfortable upright position when you meditate, although some formal meditations ask you to lie down. It is usual to close your eyes when you practice formal meditation, to help you focus, and to use a clock to keep time. Many people find that it is best to start small. For example, you could begin with a simple three-minute meditation. You could then slowly increase it to five, ten, or fifteen minutes. When it becomes familiar, you may choose to pursue a sustained meditation for a longer period of time, say, up to one hour. It can be useful to follow a guided meditation recording at first, to help you become more familiar with what mindfulness is and how to do it.

Informal mindfulness practice, by contrast, is when you engage with your daily activities in a mindful way. You may be on the bus, cooking, eating, or walking mindfully, for example. You do not need to take time out to do this, and you do not need to close your eyes. On the contrary, informal mindful awareness can be practiced whatever you are doing, anywhere and at any time that suits you. You can be informally mindful for as long as you want to.

Mindfulness is a natural human ability that can be cultivated

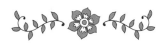

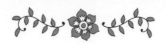

with guidance, practice, trust, and patience. It may seem simple, but many people find that it is not easy. You may find it hard to hold the focus of your attention, or you may question whether you are "doing it right," and your mind may be easily distracted. Pay attention to how you respond to yourself in such moments. There is no need to criticize yourself or judge your experience negatively. Mindfulness is a skill, and, like any new skill, it takes practice to cultivate. Remind yourself that you are paying attention to the present moment as best you can, and practice attending to yourself and your experiences with an attitude of kindness and curiosity instead. With time, the skill and art of mindfulness can become a new way of relating to yourself and your environment. It can be incorporated into your daily life as much or as little as you like.

Mindfulness and Coloring

Coloring is one enjoyable, creative way of incorporating mindfulness into your life. Naturally, coloring, drawing, painting, and other creative pursuits have a great deal in common with mindfulness meditation. Like mindfulness, they too involve awareness, making conscious choices, finding focus, connecting with the body, curiosity, going with the flow, and

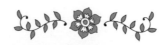

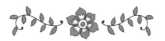

becoming absorbed in an activity with a childlike ease of being. They can evoke feelings of living in the now, simply being, enjoyment, fulfilment, and calm. They can also activate our expectations and critical judgements, which can be managed effectively with a mindful mind.

This book offers you an introduction to some of the fundamental principles of mindfulness. It also provides the opportunity to practice mindfulness via coloring. Each page of coloring is accompanied by an exercise that will enhance your understanding of what mindfulness is and how to do it. Some of the exercises will assist specifically with your experience of mindful coloring. Others will teach you more general mindfulness skills that you can practice before or while you are coloring. There are also inspirational quotes, "mindful moments" that can be used like mantras, and spaces to write your thoughts and feelings. Ultimately, this book is designed to promote your well-being. It is your companion, to help you harness your creativity, express yourself in color, and live mindfully—moment by moment.

With warm wishes,
Dr. Sarah Jane Arnold

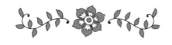

"The art of living lies in
a fine mingling of letting
go and holding on."

Havelock Ellis

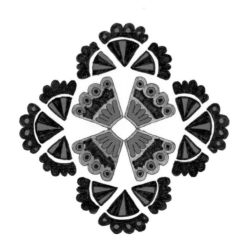

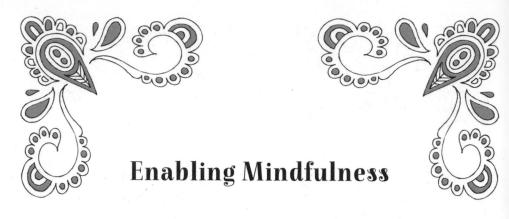

Enabling Mindfulness

Notice your intention to color, and really
look at the patterns that you see. How are
you feeling in this moment? How does your
body feel right now? Take a moment to notice
your posture. Observe your thoughts.
When you decide to color, see if you can do so
with your full attention, and with a kind, curious,
and non-judgemental attitude. Every time you
choose to color in this way, you are offering
your mind a sanctuary called mindfulness. By
practicing mindfulness, you have the opportunity
to experience each moment in your life more fully.
You can begin this experience right now.

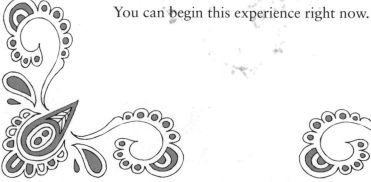

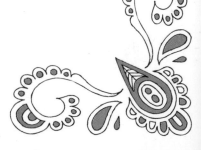

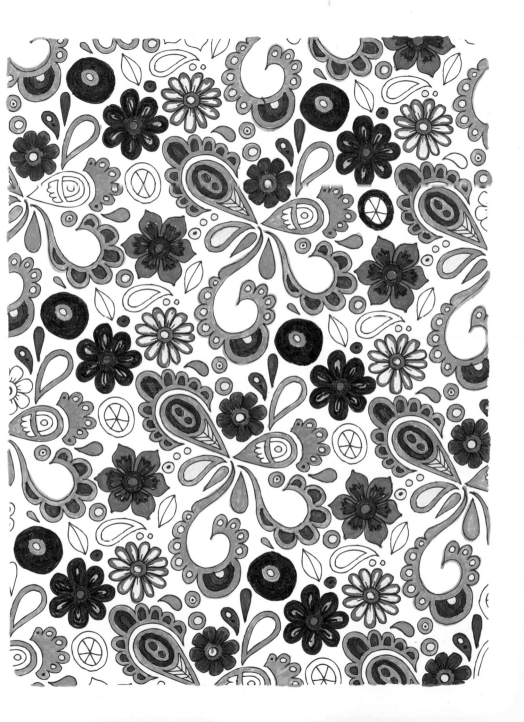

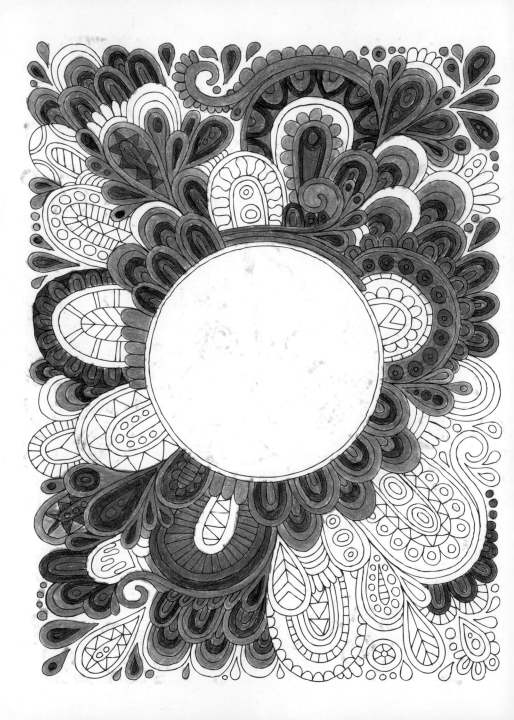

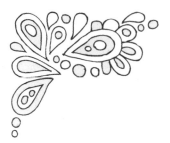
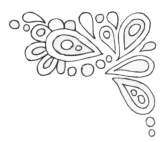

Cultivating Gratitude

Gratitude, like mindfulness, involves paying
attention to what is present with an attitude of
loving-kindness. Can you bring to mind someone
or something that you are grateful for? Take your
time. It may be an aspect of yourself, like your
eyesight. It could be someone present and positive
in your life, like a partner, parent, or friend. You
might think of an aspect of your life, such as
where you live. Write down what comes to mind
in the space provided in the pattern opposite, and
rest in the warmth of this feeling for a while.
Begin to color when you wish, and
allow gratitude to be with you.

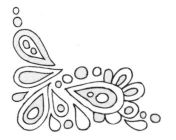

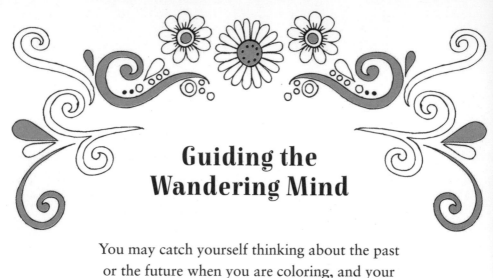

Guiding the Wandering Mind

You may catch yourself thinking about the past
or the future when you are coloring, and your
mind may flit from thought to thought. If this
happens, there is no need to judge yourself—we
can be easily distracted. Simply notice where
your mind has gone and bring the focus of
your attention back to the present moment.
Focus on an aspect of your experience right
now, and allow it to take center stage in your
awareness. For example, you could look at the
piece you are coloring, and pay attention to your
breathing. With kindness to yourself, repeat
this exercise whenever your mind wanders.

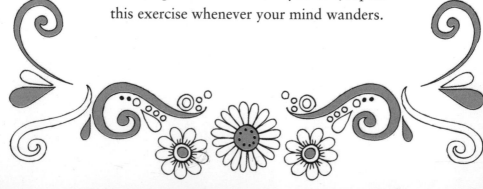

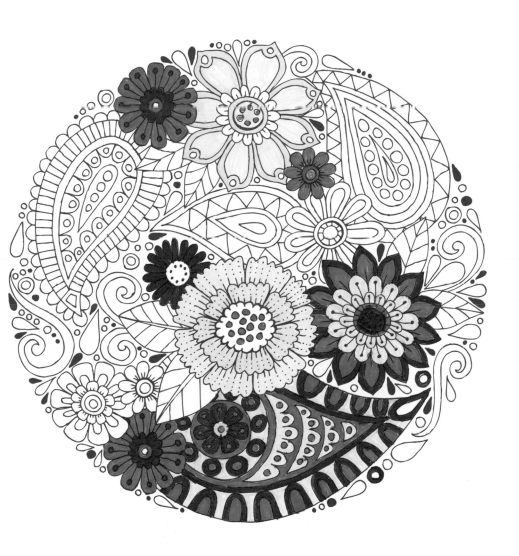

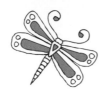

A Mindful Moment

I can observe and
guide my mind.

Reflections:

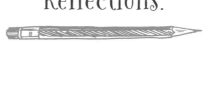

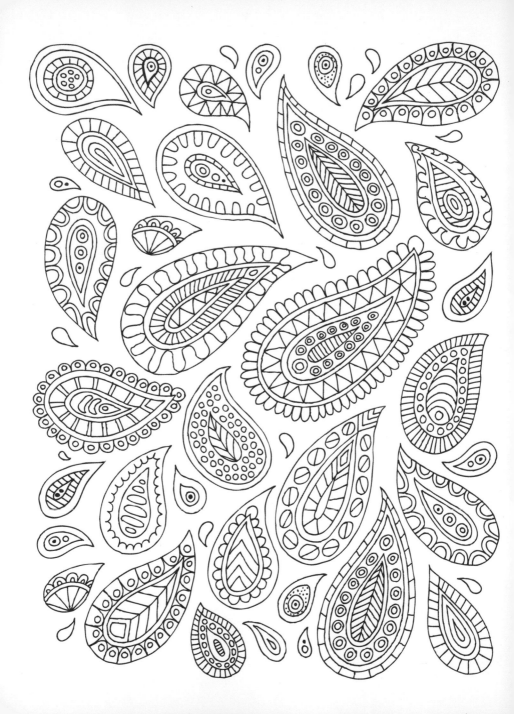

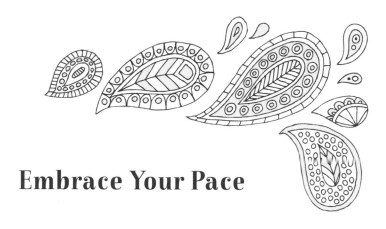

Embrace Your Pace

Take this opportunity to play mindfully with
the speed of your coloring. Experiment!
Color very, very slowly for a few minutes,
and then color incredibly fast. Allow yourself
to be curious. Notice as any thoughts
arise in your mind about this experience.
Observe them, and then let them go.
Now, color at a pace that feels comfortable
for you. Tune in to yourself and simply
go with the flow. Become aware of how it
feels for you to move at your own pace.
Embrace this way of being right now.

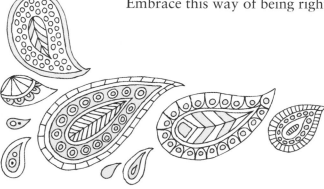

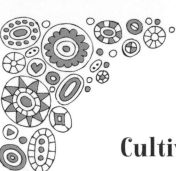

Cultivating Curiosity

As you color, practice "pressing pause" at
various points. Do this at least several times
and exercise your instinctual curiosity in the
moments that follow. Pause to look around you
and absorb what your senses are experiencing.
Pause again to notice the colors that you are
using. Consider their shade and tone, and look
at them intently. Notice the position of your
dominant hand and how it feels where it rests.
What will it feel like to sit somewhere
else and color the rest of this pattern?
Try it, and observe your experience.
Marvel at the richness of any given moment
when you pause to notice what exists.

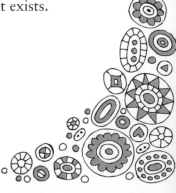

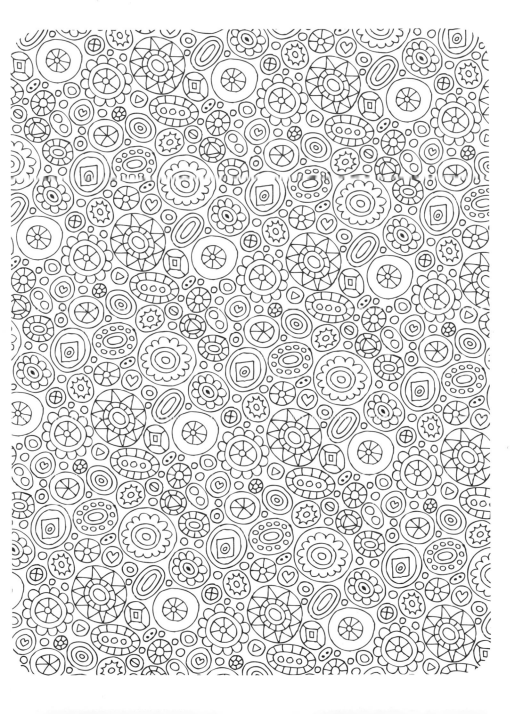

"Knowing yourself is the beginning of all wisdom."

Aristotle

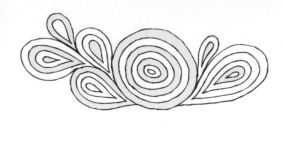

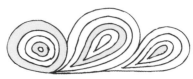

Mindful Breathing

Before you begin to color, pay attention to yourself breathing in this moment. See if you can breathe gently, in and out. Sit comfortably and close your eyes for a moment. Allow your full attention to be directed to your breathing. Become aware of how the air feels as it passes in and out through your nose or mouth. Notice its temperature and any scents in the air. Notice how it fills your lungs and your chest as you breathe. Now, open your eyes and begin to color when you wish. Breathe in the vitality of the present moment while you color.

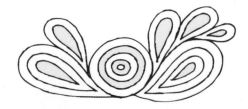

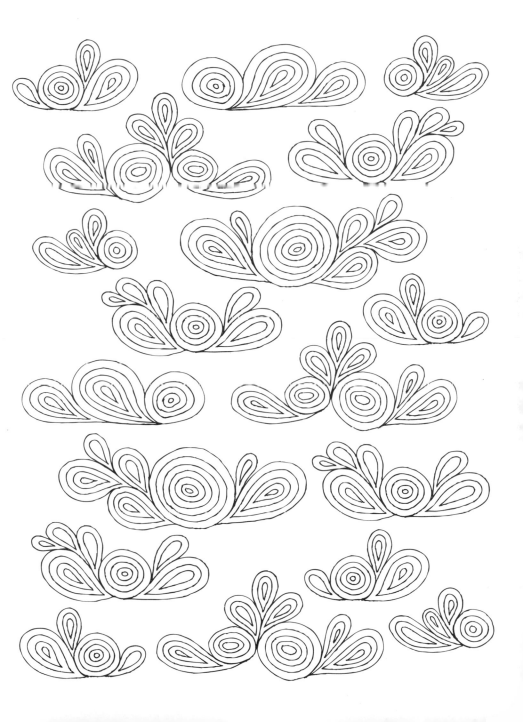

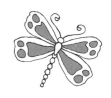

A Mindful Moment

Breathe in the now.

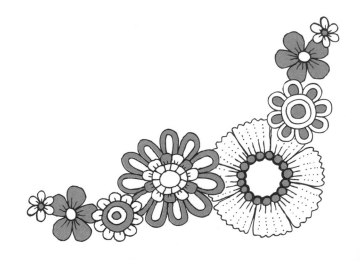

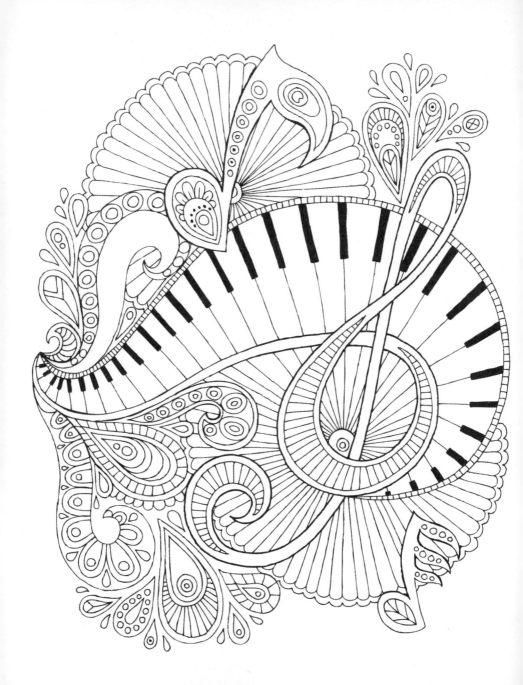

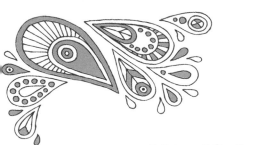
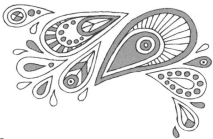

Mindful Coloring
With Music

Take this time for yourself and put on some of your
favorite music. It may be one song, an album, or
a playlist that will last for hours. When you are
ready to color and are sitting comfortably, press
play. As you color, welcome the music into your
body and mind. Allow it to flow through you
like the color flows from the end of your colored
pencil or pen. Notice the details and richness
in the music that you are listening to and in the
design that you can see. Maybe write down some
of the lyrics that stand out to you. Your senses are
alive in this moment. Simply go with the flow.

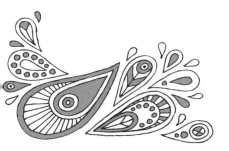
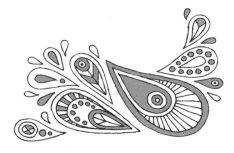

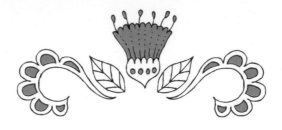

Color Your Emotions

Take a moment and check in with yourself before
you color the pattern opposite. What emotions
are you currently feeling? Do you have colors
that represent these emotions? If you do, perhaps
you could use these colors and create with them.
Welcome each emotion that you are feeling just as
you welcome each new color onto the page, and
simply see what arises. Look upon your creation
with curiosity, compassion, and loving-kindness,
and practice accepting each and every emotion
that you notice. This is your experience right now,
and you are allowed to feel the way that you do.

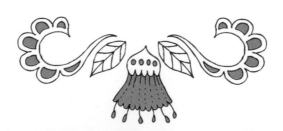

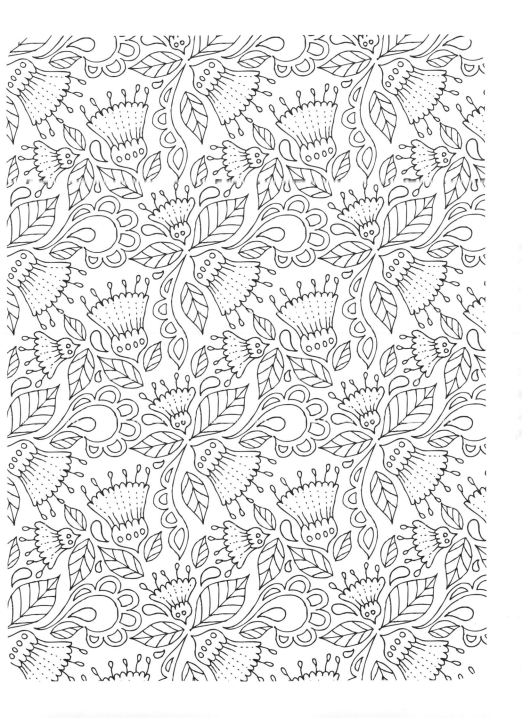

"Be curious, not judgemental."

Walt Whitman

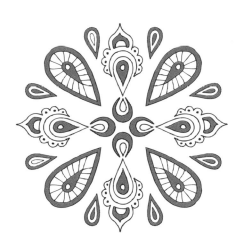

Self-compassion

See if you can bring to mind the name of a person or a pet that you care about and who cares about you. This is a being that brings you joy. Rest your mind in this place of compassion and loving-kindness for a minute or two, and then write their name within the space opposite. See if you can make room for these feelings while you color, and then offer yourself this love and kindness. You are important and worthy of such affection too.

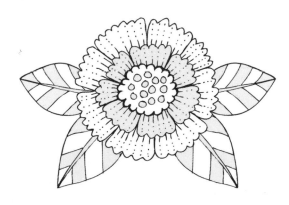

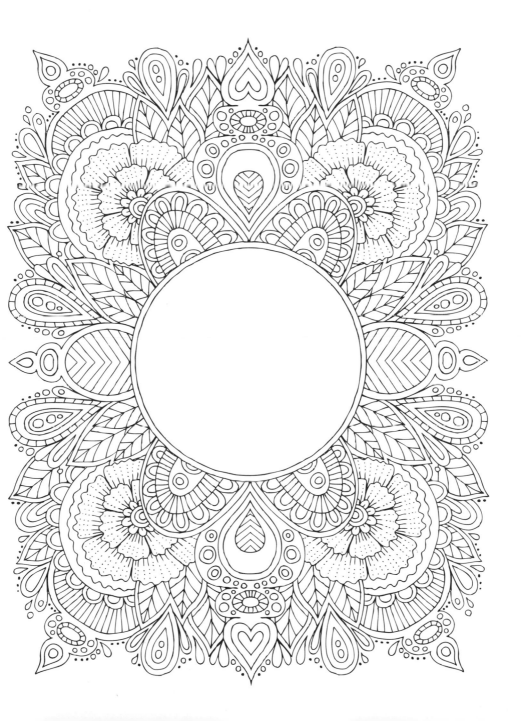

A Mindful Moment

Rest in compassion.

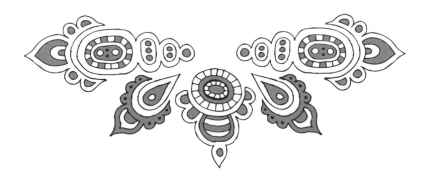

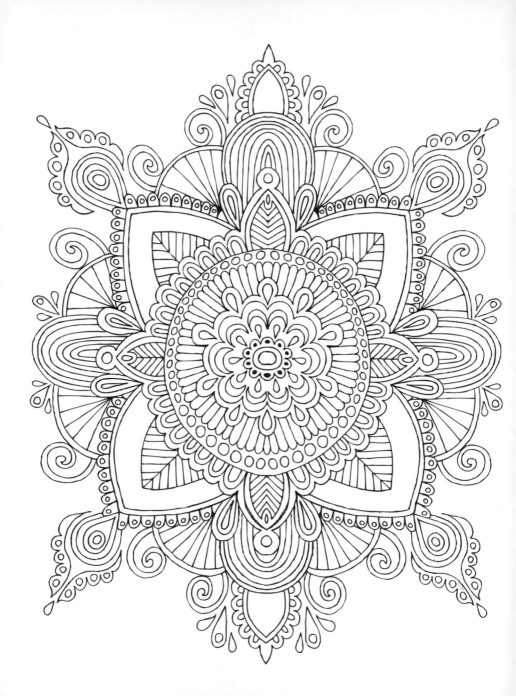

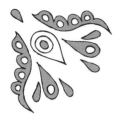
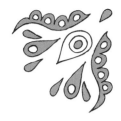

Mandala Meditation

Focus your attention and affection on the
mandala before you. Breathe gently, in and out,
and observe its center, symmetry, and intricacies.
Color at your own pace and welcome the image
of the mandala into your mind. Notice how
interconnected the lines are. Each part has its
place and connection with the other parts. Each
part adds something to the picture to make it
whole. Like you, it is beautifully multifaceted.
As you infuse your mandala with color, allow
your mind to rest in this sense of wholeness
and connection. Welcome all the different
parts of yourself and express them in color.

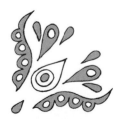
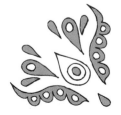

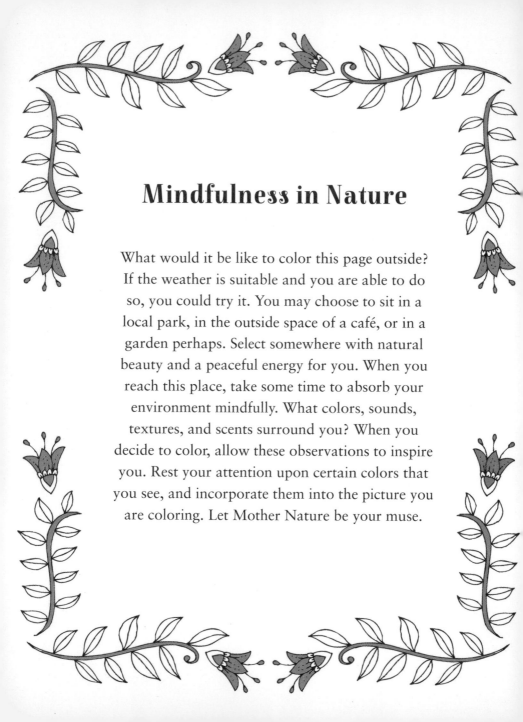

Mindfulness in Nature

What would it be like to color this page outside?
If the weather is suitable and you are able to do
so, you could try it. You may choose to sit in a
local park, in the outside space of a café, or in a
garden perhaps. Select somewhere with natural
beauty and a peaceful energy for you. When you
reach this place, take some time to absorb your
environment mindfully. What colors, sounds,
textures, and scents surround you? When you
decide to color, allow these observations to inspire
you. Rest your attention upon certain colors that
you see, and incorporate them into the picture you
are coloring. Let Mother Nature be your muse.

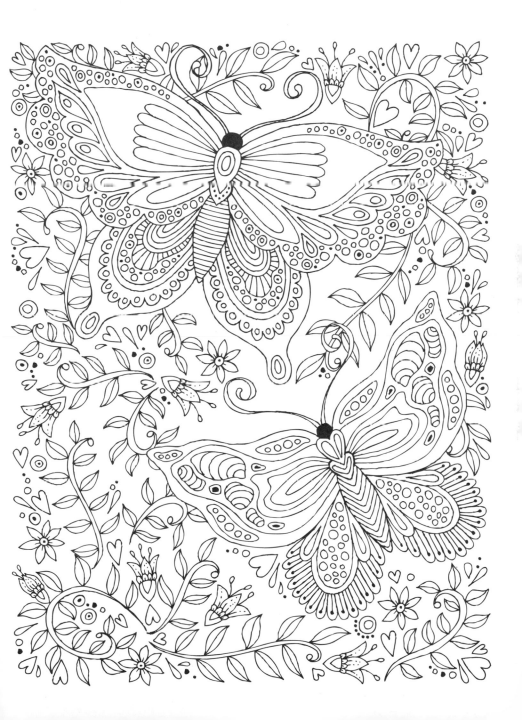

"The art of being wise is knowing what to overlook."

William James

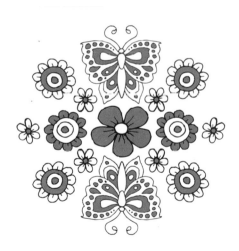

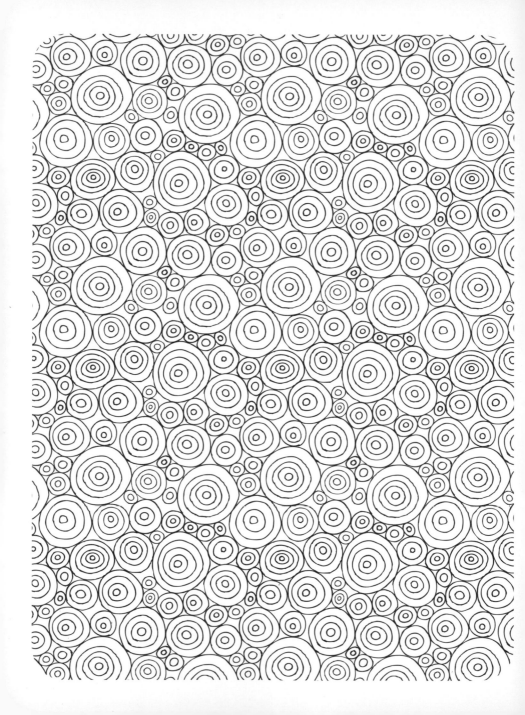

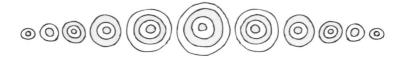

A Non-judgemental Attitude

While you are coloring, take a moment to pause and observe the picture before you. Notice the colors you have chosen and the aspects of the pattern that your mind is drawn to. Allow the picture to be just as it is, without wanting or needing things to be different. If you notice critical or judgemental thoughts, this is not a problem. Simply recognize that they have come into your mind, and then return your attention to the present moment, to the shapes and colors that you can see, and your breath as you breathe in and out. With kindness and respect, simply observe what lies before you in this moment.

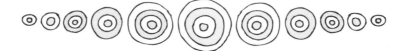

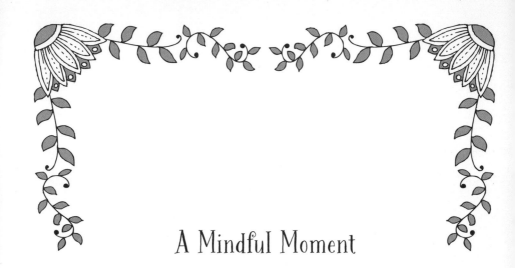

A Mindful Moment

I can choose how I respond
to my thoughts.

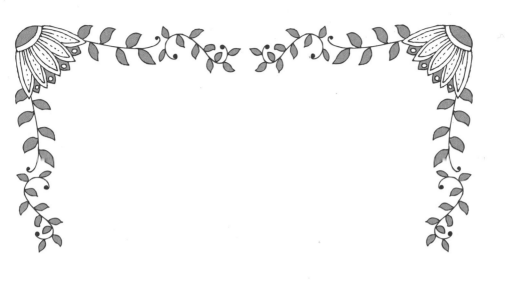
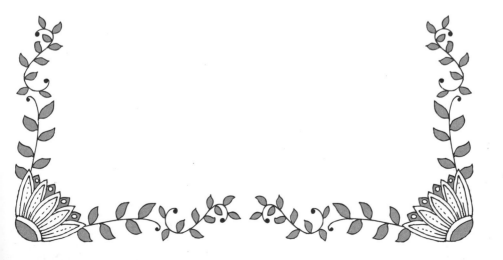

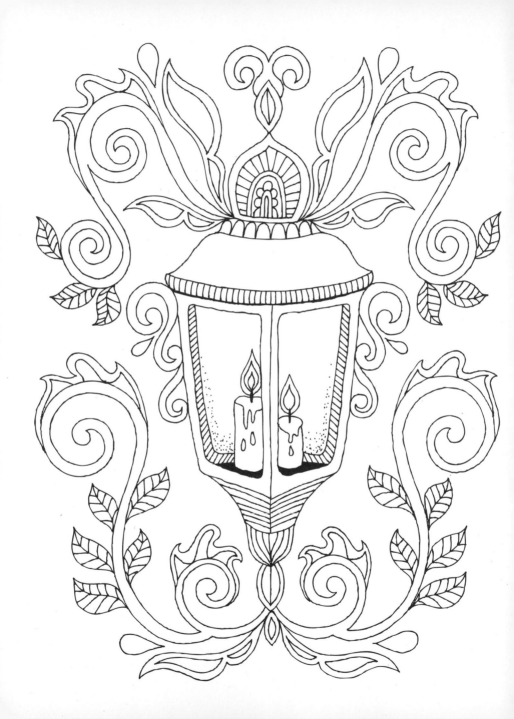

Set Your Intention

Create the intention to color this picture in a
pleasant, warm, and relaxing environment.
Consciously carve out this time for yourself,
and select a space that is quiet and peaceful.
You may wish to gather items like incense,
candles, a soft cushion, and a blanket for your
comfort. Perhaps put on some soothing music
to enhance the tranquillity of your space.
Create your setting and remind yourself of the
reason behind this: *I deserve this time, to relax
and care for myself.* Hold this kindness and
warmth with you while you color mindfully.

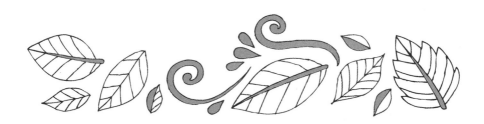

Extending Compassion and Loving-kindness

Take this opportunity to be silently mindful about someone that you care for deeply. Bring to mind three things that you like about them. Write them down if you wish, and then take some time to appreciate this person's presence in your life. Consider the faces of strangers, and see if you can extend the warmth that you feel for your loved ones to these people too. We were all unknown to each other once. As you color the mandala before you, imagine the compassion you feel extending to all living beings. Feel loving-kindness expand with the colors that you add to the page.

May we all be happy, safe, and free from suffering.

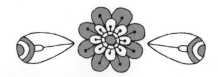

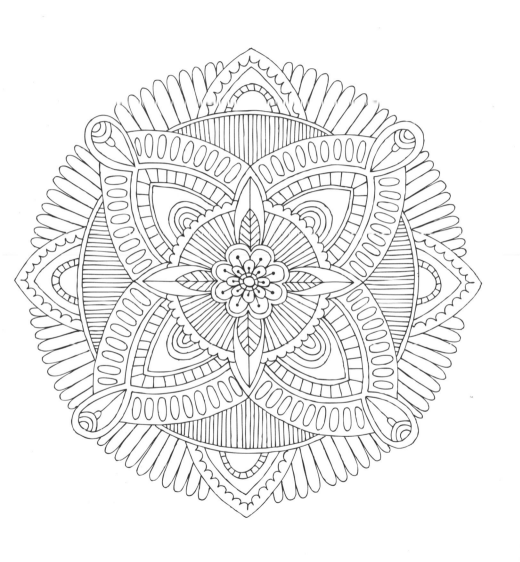

"When a painful or even a pleasant feeling arises, the Truth is—it is there. Any resistance, trying to control, wishing it away with thoughts, or fighting that feeling in any way, only causes more suffering to arise."

The Venerable U Vimalaramsi

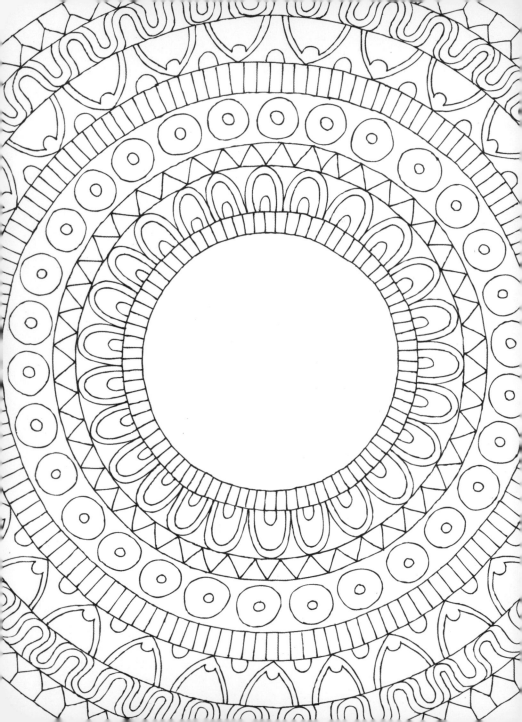

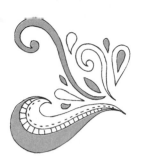
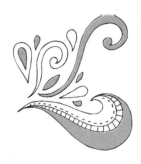

Cultivating Acceptance

How are you feeling in this moment? Use one
word to describe each emotion that you are
experiencing—for example, "thoughtful,"
"concerned," and "hopeful"—and write them in
the space provided in the pattern opposite. See if
you can make room for these feelings to be, just
as they are. Simply name them and acknowledge
that they are there. You do not need to like
them. Remind yourself that you are allowed
to feel this way, even if it is uncomfortable.
Now, see if you can shift the focus of your attention
to the pattern before you, and color when you
wish. This moment is meaningful and it is yours.

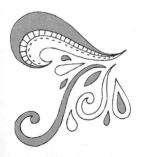

Reflections:

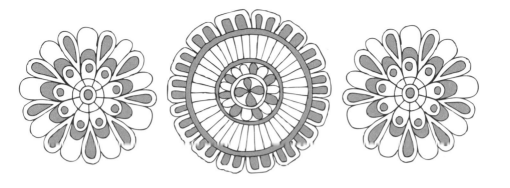

A Mindful Moment

I can tolerate the
emotions that I feel.

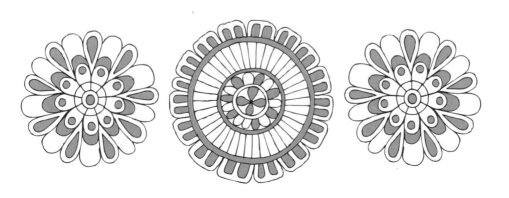

Coming Home
to Yourself

Close your eyes and gently bring the focus of your
attention to the center of your forehead. Allow
your eyes to rest in this direction—in this safety,
in this place—as you breathe gently in and out at
your own pace. Just breathe. This is your sanctuary.
You are coming home to yourself, moment by
moment, with every breath. If your mind wanders,
notice this with kindness and simply refocus your
attention back to the center of your forehead,
with your eyes closed. Keep breathing mindfully.
Notice how you feel when you decide to open
your eyes, and begin to color when you wish.

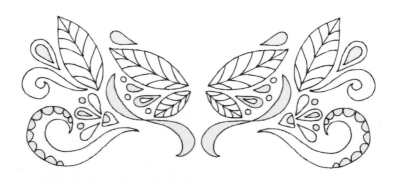

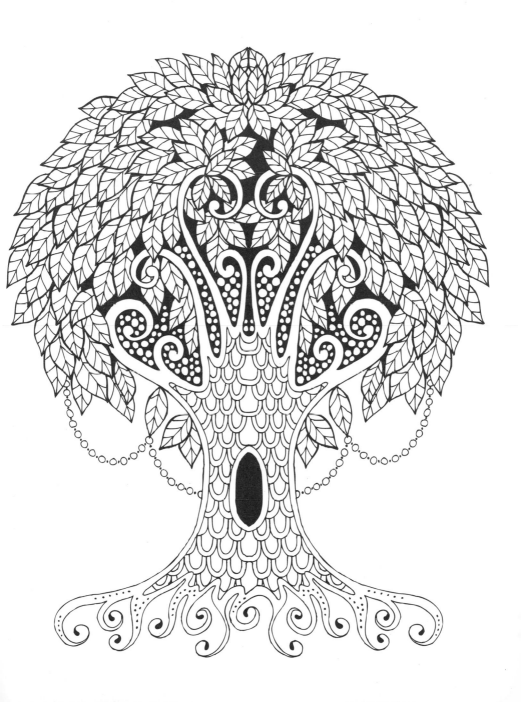

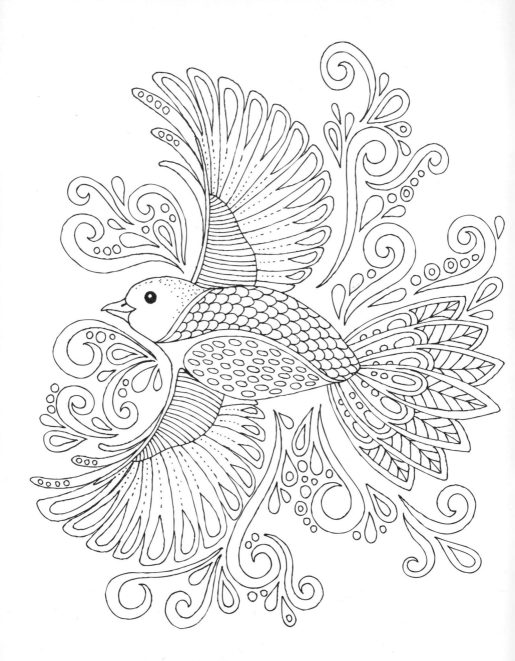

Release

Before you color, hold both of your hands out
before you and squeeze them as tightly as you
can. Hold them tensed in this position for three
seconds, and then release them. Now do it again.
Clench your fists, and then release. Notice the
tension leaving your body when your hands
open. Let it go, and welcome how your hands
feel without it. Allow any tension to flow out
through your hands as you color. Release it. There
is no need to hold it with you in this moment.

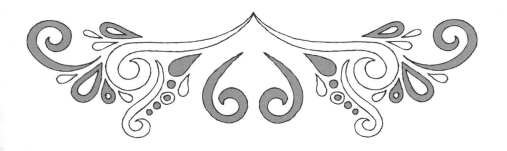

"The real voyage of discovery consists not in seeking new landscapes, but in having new eyes."

Marcel Proust

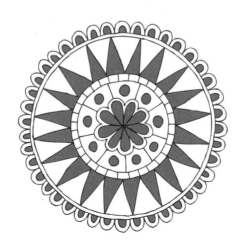

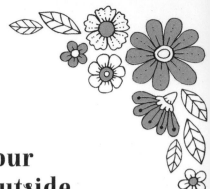

Direct Your Attention Outside

Consciously direct your attention to the environment that surrounds you right now, and tune in to the various things that you can see, hear, touch, taste, and smell before you begin to color. Notice life's finer details and name the things that you can perceive, without judgement. Notice how flexible your attention can be as you move your focus from one event to the next at your own pace. Moment by moment, you are living in the present and experiencing its fullness—just as it is. It is yours to embrace.

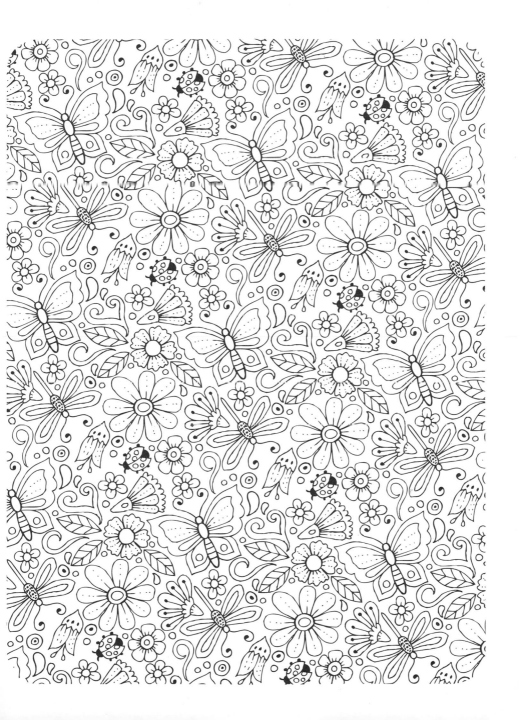

A Mindful Moment

I am deeply connected with
my external world.

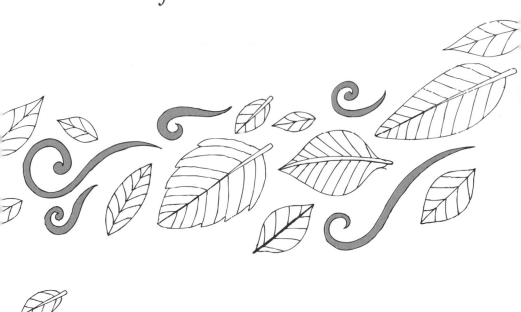

Color With Kindness

Repeat these words to yourself and
see if you can truly mean them.

In this moment, I am good enough.
In this moment, I am lovable.
In this moment, I care for myself.

Write down these words if you want
to, and make space for them to be here
with you now while you color.

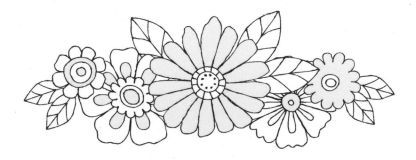

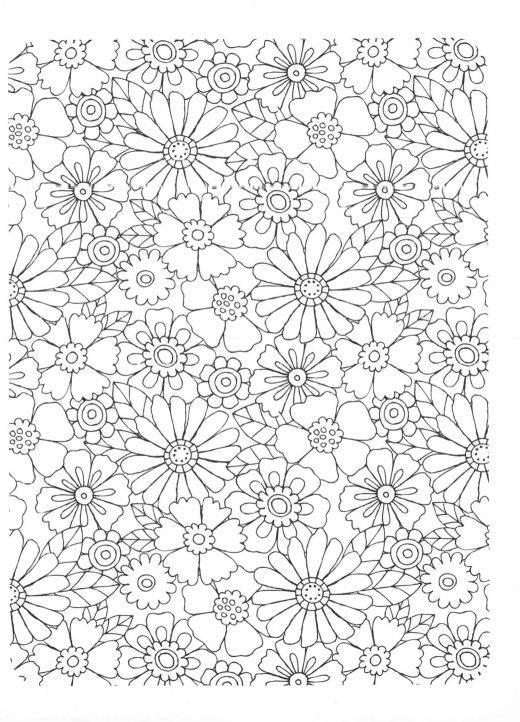

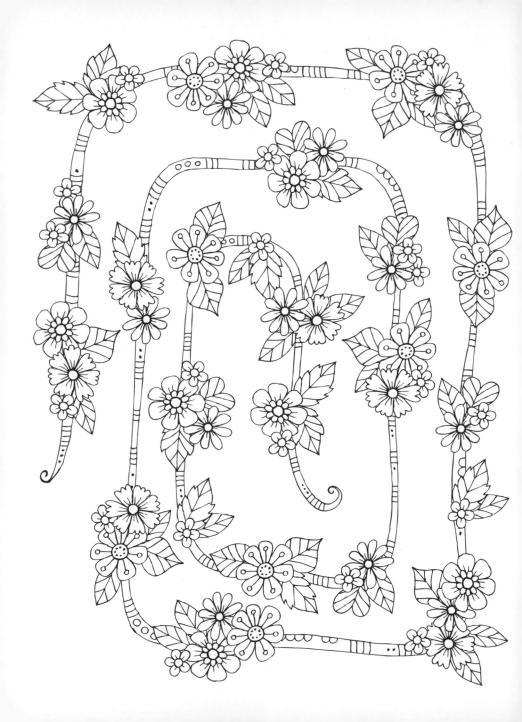

Focus With Curiosity and Patience

What is it like to try to color with your non-dominant hand? That is, the opposite hand from the one you usually use. See if you can use this hand only, and focus your attention on coloring in this way. Notice how much patience and concentration it requires. It may feel very new and unfamiliar. It may even feel frustrating. Notice and name any emotions that arise, moment by moment, and allow them to be here with you as you try to guide your hand as it colors. See if you can experience this without making any judgements. Notice how present you are in this moment.

"I can alter my life by altering my attitude. He who would have nothing to do with thorns must never attempt to gather flowers."

Henry David Thoreau

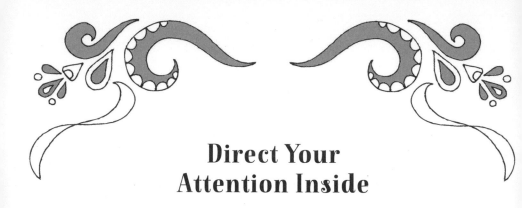

Direct Your Attention Inside

Are there any sensations within you right now? Any thoughts or feelings that you can identify? Practice noticing and naming any emotions and sensations that you feel in this moment, before you begin to color. Acknowledge your thoughts as thoughts by recognizing them and saying to yourself, "I'm having a thought that ..." Then return your attention to your breathing, and begin to color when you wish. In this mindful moment, you can view your internal landscape from a distance with clarity. There is space for you to breathe here. You can see as far as the horizon.

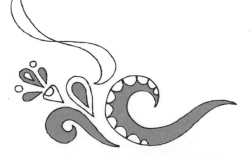
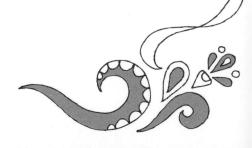

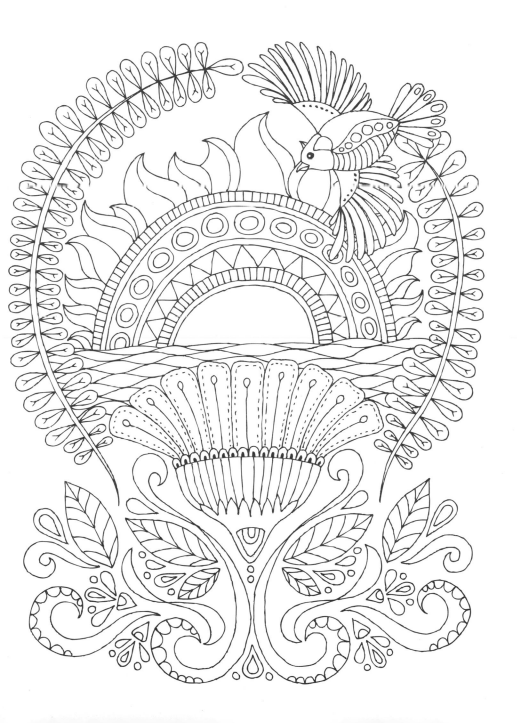

A Mindful Moment

My internal experiences
do not control me. I am
their observer.

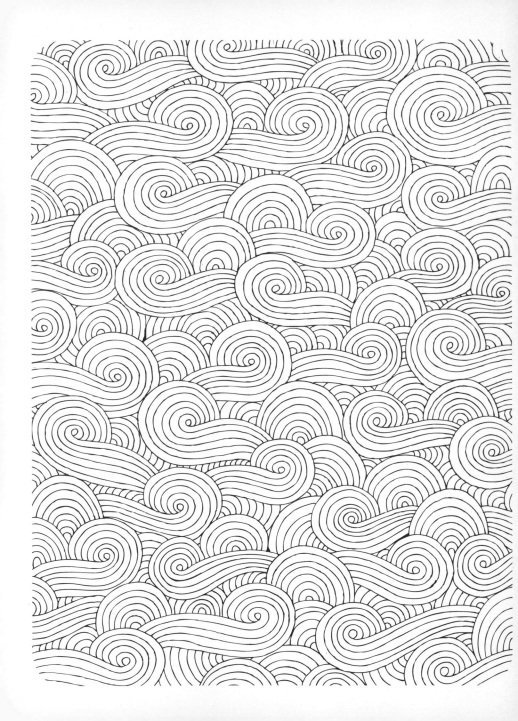

In a Challenging Moment ...

Save this exercise for a moment when you
are feeling emotionally challenged.

*In this moment, I can name and allow the emotions
that I am feeling.* Go ahead, write them down.

----

*In this moment, I can observe the thoughts running
through my mind.* Write these down, too.

----

*I am grounded in knowing myself and
my struggle in this moment.
I am human, and I care. I am allowed to feel this way.*

*I will ride these waves as they rise and
fall on this ground of mine.
I will refocus my attention when I want to and color mindfully.*

I can cope with this. It will pass.

Mindfulness of Sight

What can you see right now? What shapes,
textures and shades of light and dark colors
do you notice around you? Perhaps there are
some colors in your environment that capture
your attention. Allow your mind to go to them.
Select whichever pen or pencil you are drawn
to in this moment and begin to color. Notice
the crisp, white page and the black lines of the
picture before you. Drink in what you perceive,
moment by moment, and absorb what you enjoy.
Close your eyes for a few seconds and open them anew.
You may notice things that you did not see before.

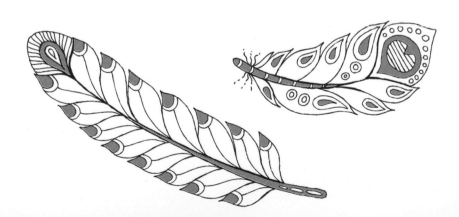

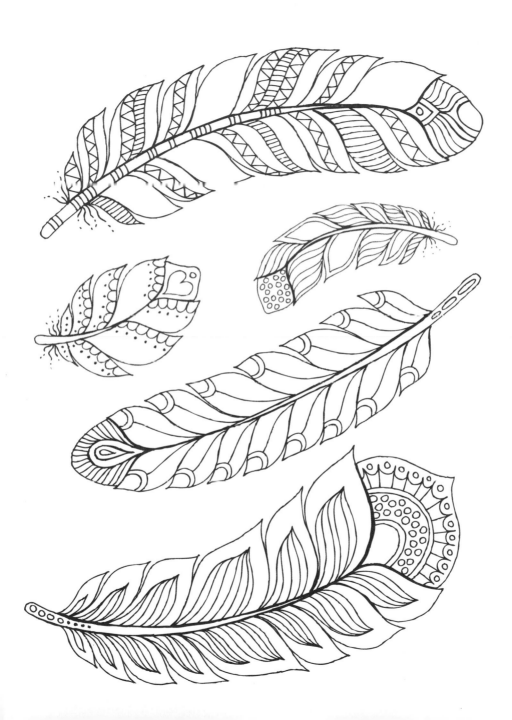

"Wherever you go,
go with all your heart."

Confucius

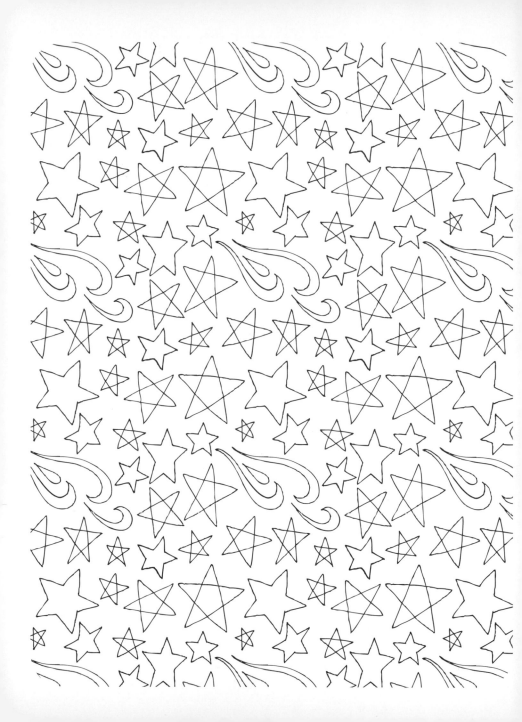

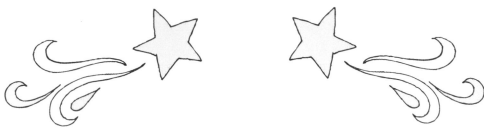

Mindfulness of
the Body

Take this time to become aware of your posture.
You may wish to adopt an alert yet comfortable
sitting position with both of your feet on the
floor. You are grounded in this moment. Notice
how your eyes move as they explore the pattern
before you. Observe your arm moving as you
color, and your hand as it holds the pen or
pencil that you have chosen. Become aware
of your breath filling your lungs and chest as
you breathe and create. Your mind and body
are deeply connected in these moments.

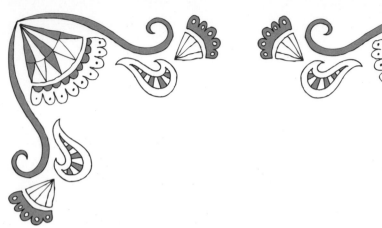
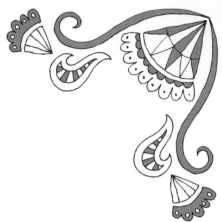
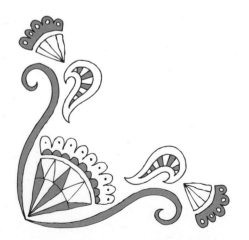
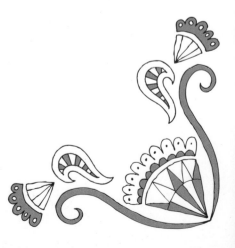

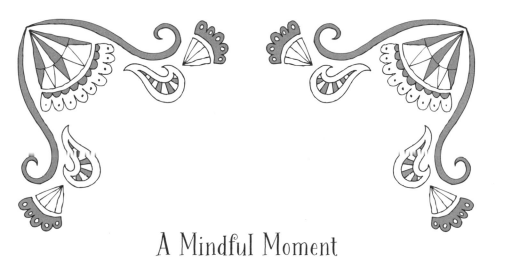

A Mindful Moment

In this moment, I am whole.

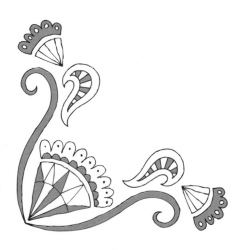
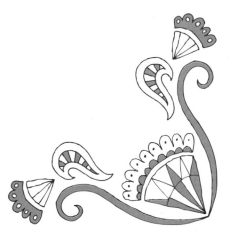

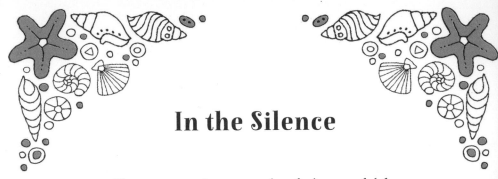

In the Silence

Choose an environment that feels peaceful for
you. One that is free from background noise,
people talking, demands, and interruptions.
Turn off your mobile phone and notice how
the silence sounds. Just listen. What can you
hear? Register and allow any sounds that you
perceive to wash over you, and tune in to your
experience of this moment. Mindfully listen to
your breathing. Notice the sounds that your
pen or pencil makes when you pick it up and
place it on the paper. Listen to yourself coloring,
and notice when your mind speaks. You are the
silent observer of your experience. Allow your
thoughts to come and go while you immerse
yourself in coloring. There is peace for you here.

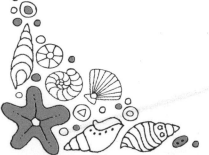
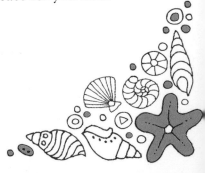

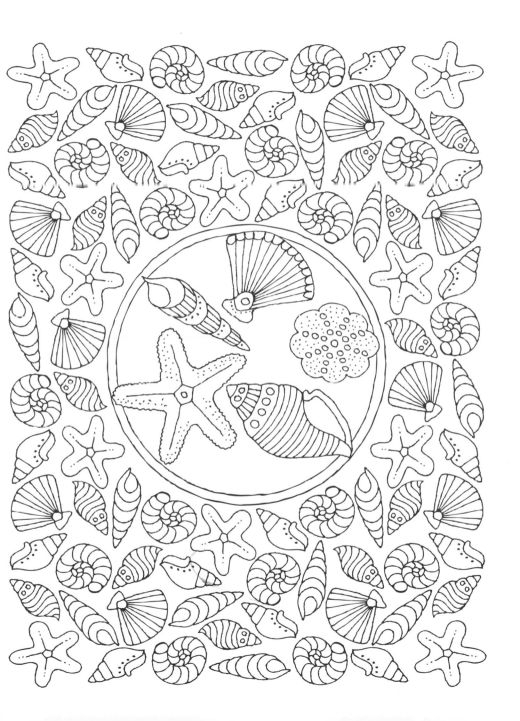

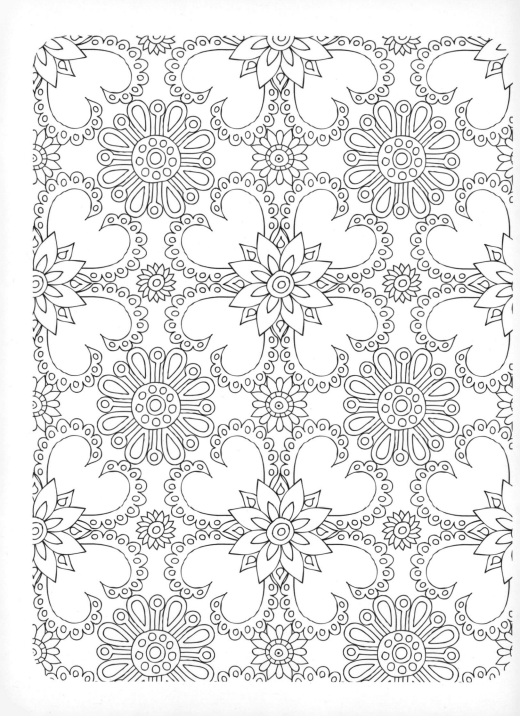

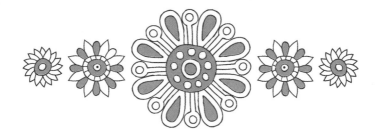

Freedom to Be

In this time, in this space, you are invited to mindfully *be*. There is no pressure on you here and there are no expectations. There is no "right" and no "wrong" way to color the pattern before you. You can choose which colors you use. You can choose how long to color for. You can decide how you color, and you can set your own pace. Inhabit each moment as it unfolds, and allow your mind the freedom to simply be. Become absorbed and immersed in your own experience of coloring.

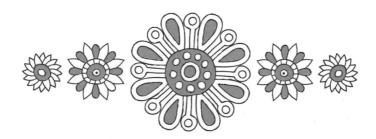

"To see a World in a
grain of sand,
And a Heaven in a
wild flower,
Hold Infinity in the
palm of your hand,
And Eternity in an hour."

William Blake

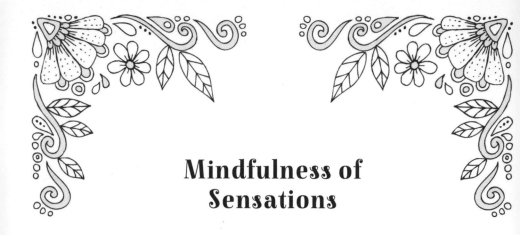

Mindfulness of Sensations

Take this moment to notice any sensations within your body right now. Observe where each feeling is and acknowledge its presence. Watch as sensations come and go and change. See if you can observe them with curiosity and openness, without wanting or needing things to be different from how they are right now. As you breathe gently, in and out, see if you can make space for these sensations. Allow them to be here with you while you color, just as they are, and expand your awareness around them.

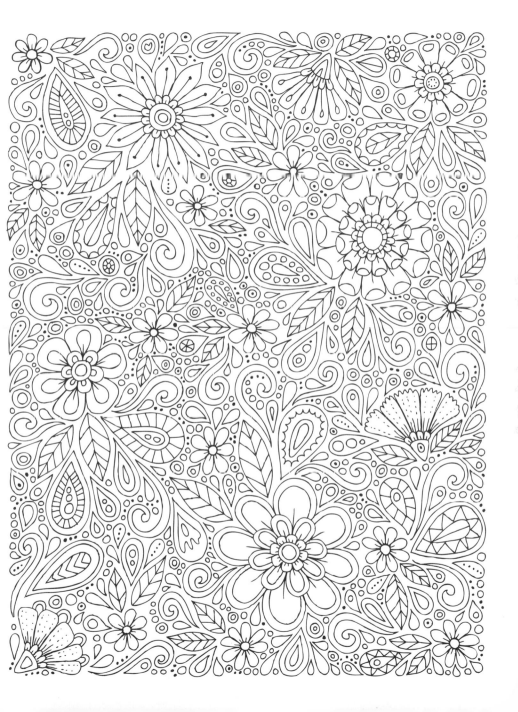

Reflections:

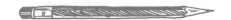

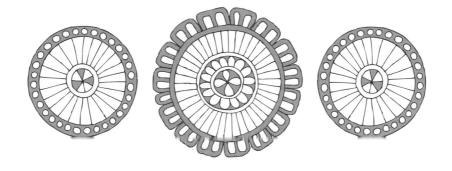

A Mindful Moment

I can observe the
sensations that I feel, and
I can see past them.

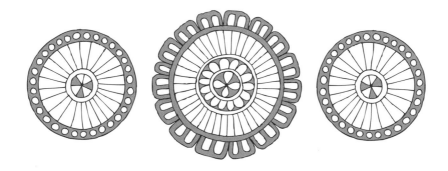

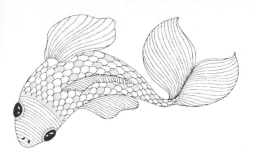

A Coloring Meditation

Settle in a comfortable place and smile at your decision to take this time for yourself. This is for you. Study the picture that you will color and really look at it. When you are ready, select your palette and begin to color mindfully. Breathe into your experience of coloring each contour, and see if you can use all of your five senses to savor each moment as it unfolds. If your mind wanders, simply note where it has gone and gently escort it back to the present moment with kindness and patience. As your pen or pencil connects with the page, feel yourself reconnect with the present moment. This is your sanctuary.

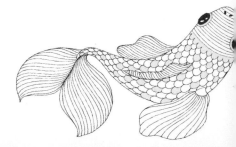

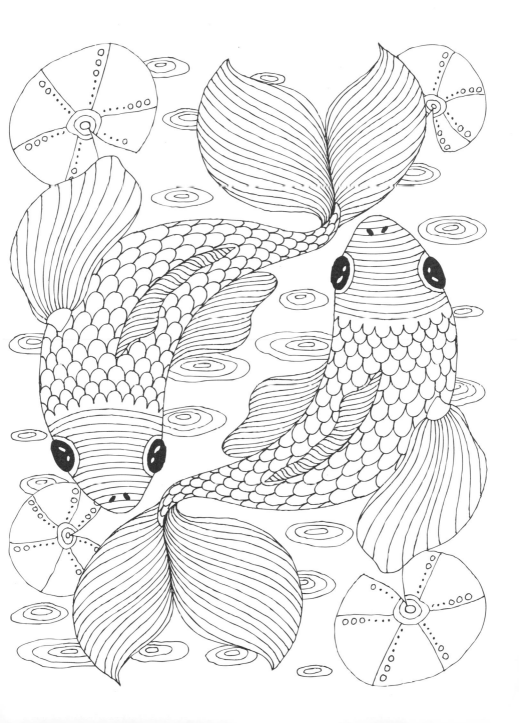

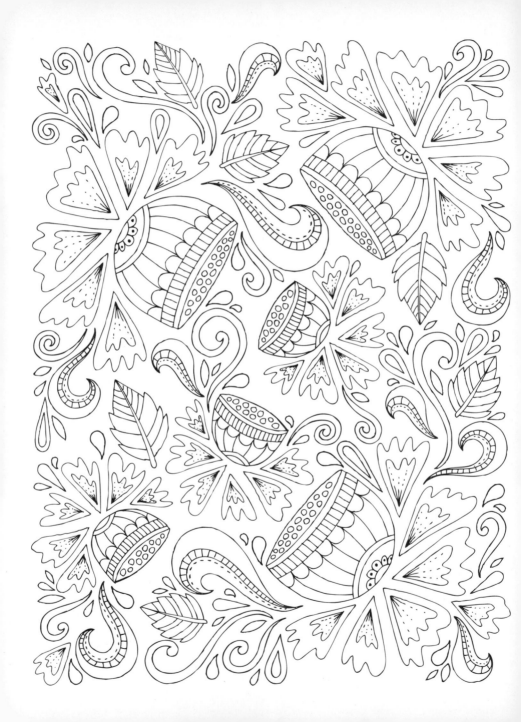

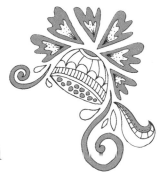

Contemplation

Before you color the next pattern, take a moment
or two to reflect upon some of the things that
make this mindful coloring experience possible
for you. Allow your mind to be touched and
inspired by the existence of everyday objects like
paper, and colored pens and pencils. Allow the
people that created these things to be in your
awareness, too. Take a moment to think about
the artist who designed the pattern that you are
choosing to color, and marvel at the ability of
your mind and body to fill it with color. Notice
how ordinary things can become extraordinary
when you contemplate them mindfully.

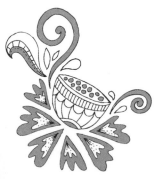
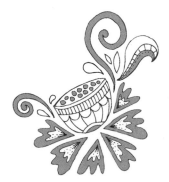

"Always hold fast to the present.
Every situation, indeed every
moment, is of infinite value,
for it is the representative
of a whole eternity."

Johann Wolfgang von Goethe

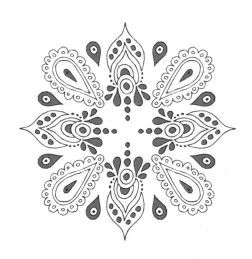

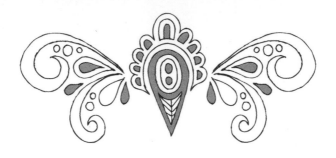

Living in the Moment

Pause in this moment and notice your breathing.
With each breath, you are creating space for
yourself to be—just as you are. In this space,
you are inviting your inner world and outer
world to be here with you now—just as they are.
Immerse yourself in coloring whenever you wish.
If you notice that you have drifted off into your
thoughts, patiently escort your mind back to your
experience of coloring. Reclaim now for yourself
and watch it unfold in color, moment by moment.

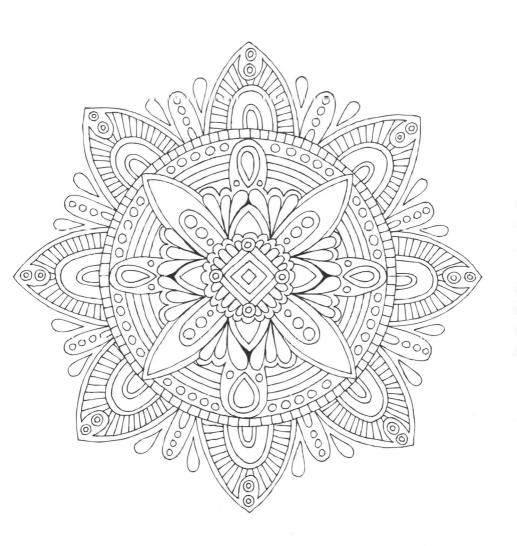

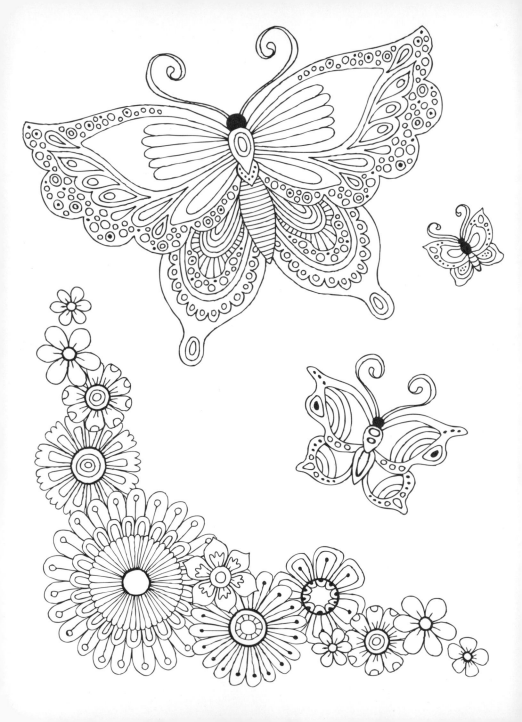

A Mindful Moment

Color in the now.

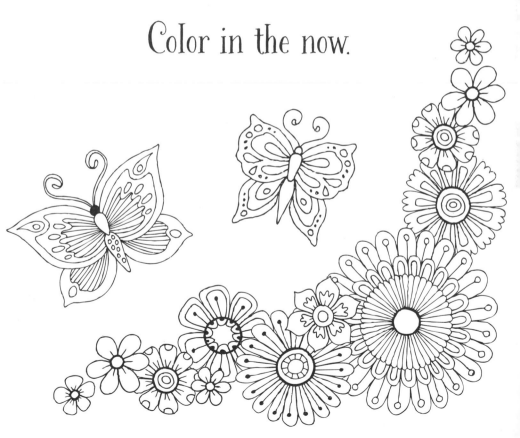

Observing Change

Observe your experience of coloring this pattern,
moment by moment. Notice each small change
that occurs with every new mark that you
make and every color that you add. Witness
the picture evolve as you fill it with color, and
acknowledge your role in creating the changes
that you see. See if you can be aware of your
internal landscape as it changes, too. Observe
your thoughts and allow them to come and go.
Make space for your emotions while you color,
too, and notice if they change, without judgement.
Savor each moment and embrace each "now."

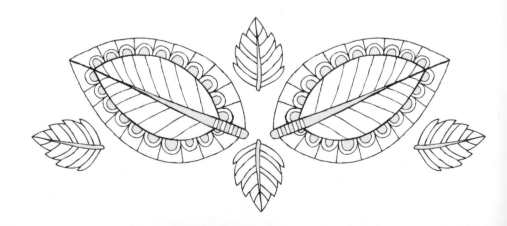

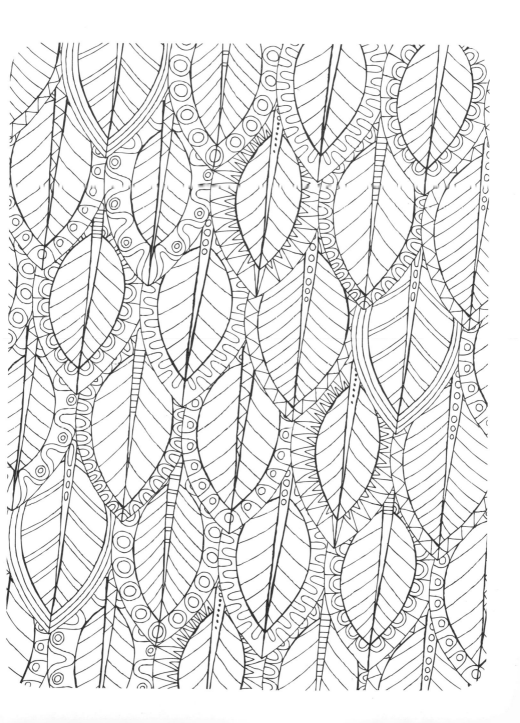

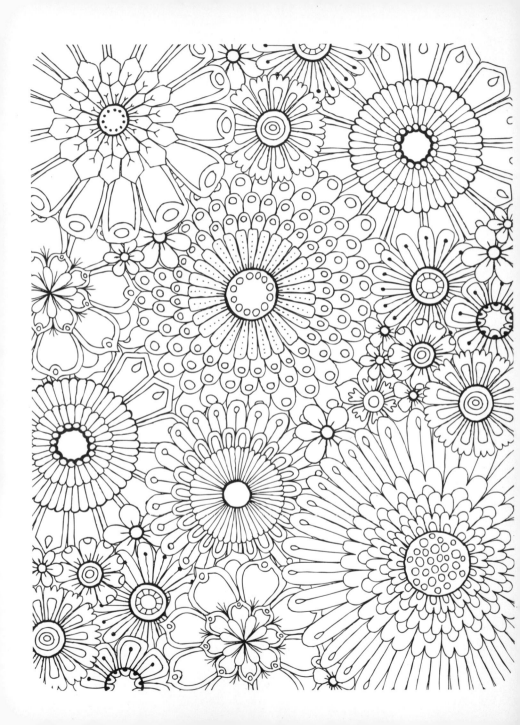

Mindfulness for Self-awareness

Witness the thoughts that come and go from your mind
while you are coloring. Write them down and return
your attention to the present moment. Practice being
the observer of your thoughts and notice the stillness
underneath them. Feel your feelings and invite them to
be here with you now. They offer insight into your well-
being. Acknowledge and accept them as best you can.
Set aside some time to respond to your thoughts
later with kindness and curiosity. Did they contain
judgements or impulses? Were they helpful? Were
they true? How were they linked to your emotions?
Give yourself a little distance from your thoughts
and see what you can learn about yourself.

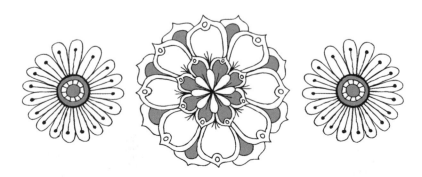

"It is in your power to withdraw yourself whenever you desire. Perfect tranquility within consists in the good ordering of the mind, the realm of your own."

Marcus Aurelius

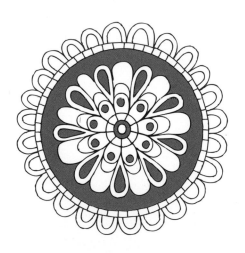

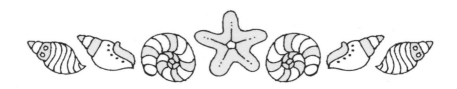

Drop Your Anchor

You may wish to practice this now, before you color. Close your eyes, if you like, and place both your feet on the floor. Breathe in through your nose for a count of four, and out through your mouth for a count of six. Do this several times. Breathe in for four, and out for six. If you drift off into your thoughts, gently escort your mind back to the present moment and anchor yourself there. Notice the feeling of your feet on the floor, your body as it moves with your breath, and the experience of gently breathing. You have the capacity to soothe and ground yourself in times of stress.

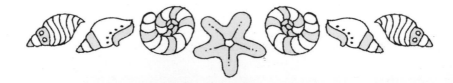

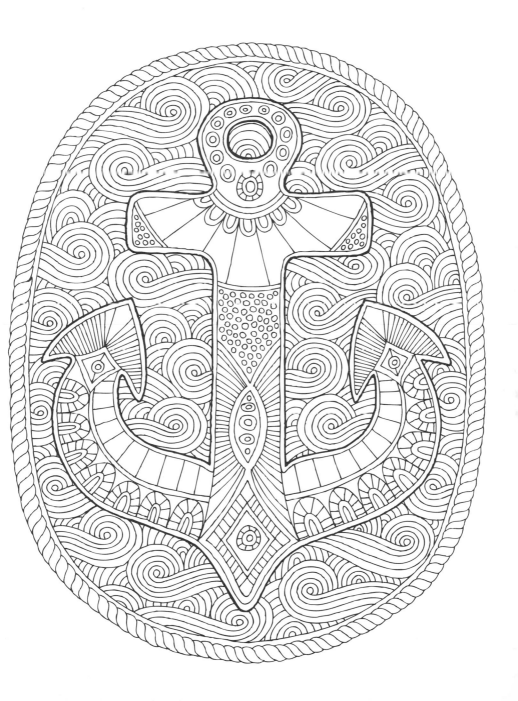

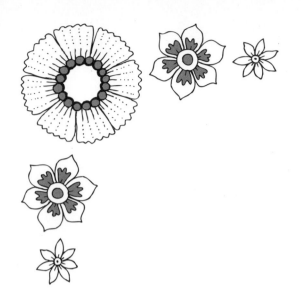
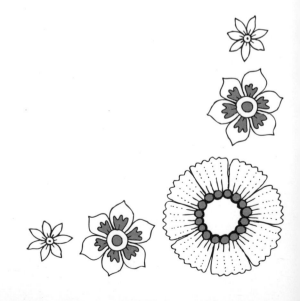

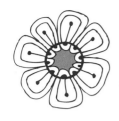
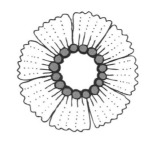

A Mindful Moment

My body and breath can anchor me now.

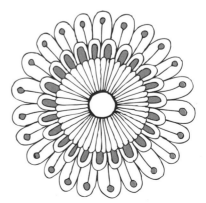

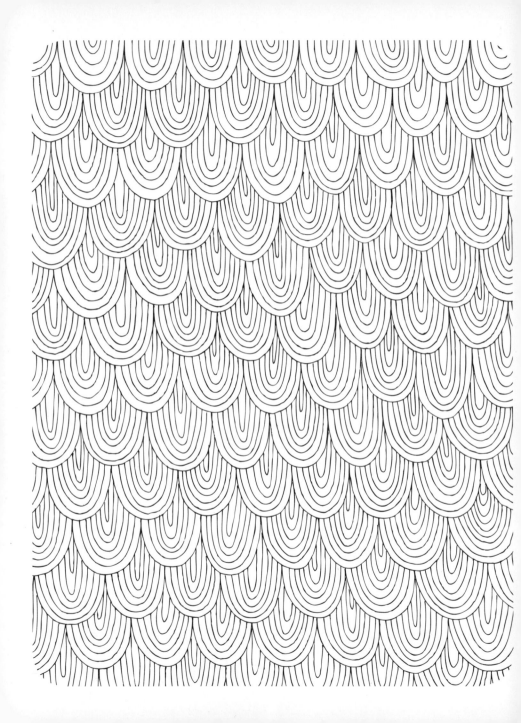

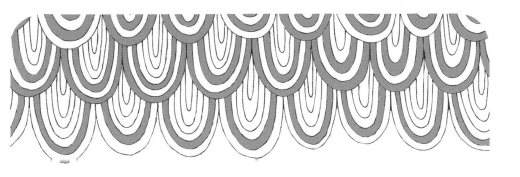

Letting Go

In this moment, there is freedom. You do not need to expect, react, hold on or strive. Simply allow the process of coloring to reveal itself to you, moment by moment. Allow your thoughts and feelings the freedom to come and go as they wish. Let them leave, and observe them as they pass by. You can explore them with perspective and clarity later if you want to. In this moment, you are choosing to embrace your experience of coloring.

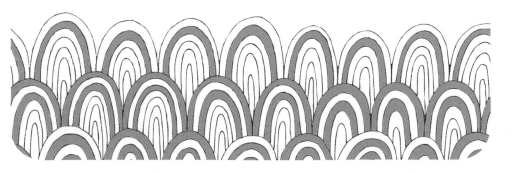

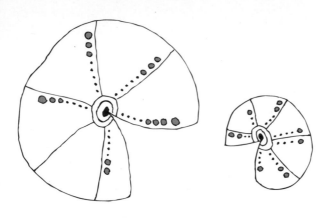

A Mindful Moment

I choose to respond, not react.

Reflections:

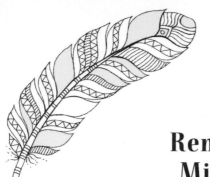

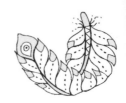

Remembering Mindfulness

Being mindful takes practice, compassion, and patience. In order to practice it, we need to remember that mindfulness is here for us to use in our everyday lives. This can be easy to forget and we can slip back into our old ways of being. If you like mindfulness, then make a conscious choice to try to hold it in your heart and mind. If you forget about it and then remember, be mindful! Offer yourself compassion and then reconnect with yourself in the present moment. Start now. Contemplate what mindfulness is and put your learning into practice as you color this final picture. Mindfulness is here for you as long as you are here.

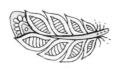

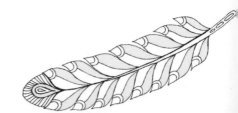

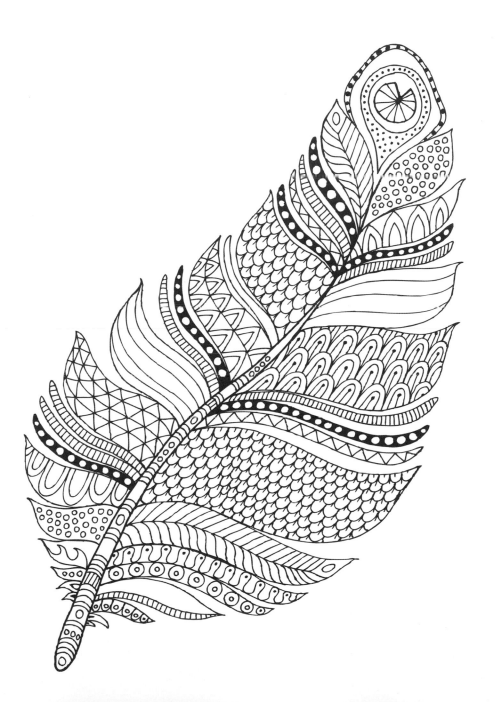

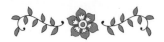

Continuing Your Journey With Mindfulness

Some useful resources:

Alidina, S. *Mindfulness for Dummies*. John Wiley & Sons Ltd, 2010.
André, C. *Mindfulness: 25 Ways to Live in the Moment Through Art*. Ebury Publishing, 2014.
Kabat-Zinn, J. *Wherever You Go, There You Are: Mindfulness Meditation in Everyday Life*. Hyperion Books, 1994.
Nhat Hanh T. *The Miracle of Mindfulness: An Introduction to the Practice of Meditation*, trans. Mobi Ho, Rider Books, 1991.
Penman, D. and Williams, M. G. *Mindfulness: A Practical Guide to Finding Peace in a Frantic World*. Hachette Digital, Little Brown Book Group, 2011.
Williams, M., Teasdale, J., Segal, Z., and Kabat-Zinn, J. *The Mindful Way Through Depression: Freeing Yourself From Chronic Unhappiness*. The Guilford Press, 2007.

For more information about what mindfulness is, how to do it, and some brilliant free guided meditations (in "Resources") go to:
www.franticworld.com

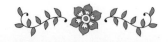

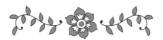

A word of caution:

It is important to state that a small proportion of people find the practice of mindfulness meditation too emotionally challenging. If this is your experience, then now may not be the right time for you to practice mindfulness without suitable support. It may be helpful to speak to a supportive mental health professional about your thoughts and feelings instead. Mindfulness will be here when the time is right for you.

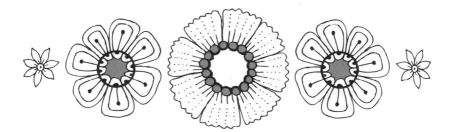

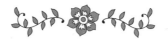

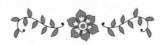

About the Author

Dr. Sarah Jane Arnold is a Chartered Counseling Psychologist. In her private practice she works with people experiencing life issues and specific mental health difficulties, to enhance their well-being via integrative, mindfulness-informed psychological therapy.

Sarah lives in Brighton, in the UK, with her partner, Mine, their dog, Oprah, and Priscilla the bearded dragon.

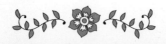